Uber and Lyft Ride Sharing NOT

Thomas J Miezejeski

Management Resource Center

Hackettstown, New Jersey, 2019

Uber and Lyft, Ride Sharing NOT 1st Edition Copyright 2019 by Thomas Miezejeski manufactured in the United States of America All Right Reserved. No part of this book may be reproduced in any form by any electronic or mechanical form including information storage and retrieval systems without permission from the publisher, except by a reviewer, who may quote brief passages in a review. Published by the Management Resource Center, 431 Mansfield Village, Hackettstown, NJ, 07840

732 267 1589

Contents

Dedication

Authors Note

Forward

Chapter 1Unintended Consequences

Chapter 2History and Current Status of Ride Sharing

Chapter 3How Does Lyft Work

Chapter 4Are You working FOR the Ride Sharing Co.

Chapter 5Income Expense and Profit

Chapter 6A Word of Caution on Insurance

Chapter 7Not Just a Taxi Service

Chapter 8Part of a Larger Economic Trend

Chapter 9Recommendations

Appendix IWhy Ride Sharing Companies will not use Self Driving Vehicles

Appendix IIInteresting Rides

About the Author

Uber and Lyft , Ride Sharing -- NOT

Dedication - To my 1000+ passengers, who made this book possible.

I am based in Northern NJ, but passenger destinations have taken me to as far east as the four boroughs of NY: Brooklyn, Bronx, Manhattan and Queens. As far North as Rockland County in NY, as far south as Camden, which is across the Delaware River from Philadelphia, and as far into Pennsylvania as 40 mile west of the Delaware Water Gap. I arrived at all of these destinations without ever getting lost once.

I lived, went to school and worked in the New York Metropolitan, also known as the tri-state area, all my life. At the risk of sounding biased, I believe that it is a very unique geographic area that has enabled me to have a diversity of experience that may not be possible in any other part of the country, Specifically, with regard to taxis, the system of medallion cabs in Manhattan has no equal.

Authors Note

I started writing this book while I was an active driver for Lyft. Since then I was hit by a deer that totaled the car I used to drive for Lyft. After I reported that accident I learned that my insurance company did not cover the accident, since I was driving for Lyft with passengers in my car. I was covered by Lyft's insurance company. I learned the hard way that the insurance provided by Lyft has a much higher deductible and does not provide for a rental car while I am waiting for my car to be repaired or I purchase a another vehicle. If I was aware of this major difference in insurance I would never have started driving for Lyft.

From the very beginning of my driving for Lyft I had some problems with Lyft's transparency with regard to the true earning potential. I cover this in detail in a separate chapter that addresses the earnings potential of being a driver for a shared ride company. I talk about Lyft in this book because I have first hand knowledge from driving for the company. While there are some differences among shared ride companies, for the most part they work the same way when it comes to compensating drivers.

Forward

The number one question that passengers ask is how do you like being a Lyft driver? There is no question that many people as just asking to make conversation during the ride, but do believe that there are a good number of people who are genuinely interested in the ride sharing phenomenon. All ride sharing companies provide many billions of rides each year, but there still many people each day who are having their first ride sharing experience. That is one of the reasons why I am writing this book.

When I started writing this book I thought I knew where my experience driving for Lyft fit in with the experience of the 4 million plus people who have also driven for a ride sharing company. Simply stated I though I had limited experience in what driving for a ride sharing is all about. I earned just over $13,000 in about nine mouths of giving just over 1000 rides. As I compiled my experience and did research into the experience of others who have worked for ride sharing companies I realized that it was a lot more extensive than I thought. Surely there are thousands of people who have earned far more money than I did, but in terms a of a percentile ranking I am much higher than I thought. Since 48 percent of all drivers for Uber earn less than $99 per month, I know that I am in the top 50 percent. Just applying the old 80 20 rule, which states that of all experiences in almost anything 20 percent of the people account for 80 percent of all experience or activity I am fairly confident that I am in the top 20 percent of all drivers.

Furthermore, while I started out driving for a ride sharing company to make a little extra money, it turned out to be a nine month long information gathering project needed to do an analysis of the ride staring business model. My day job throughout my life, if you want to call it that, has been to analyze the viability of new products and services. After I had been driving for Lyft for a month, I started to ask myself am I really making any money from this activity. Since I had been doing it for all my life why would I stop now?

Ironically and very dramatically I got my answer all in one night when I was hit by a deer while driving for Lyft with three passengers in my car. Fortunately, no one was hurt, but my car turned out to be a total loss. The buck hit me while I was driving at night on a country road, at about 50 miles per hour. Shortly after that night I learned my personal insurance company did not cover the accident rather the company that covers Lyft would cover the accident. My personal insurance provides for a $1000 deductable for a comprehensive claim, which is what a deer hit is. Lyft's carrier has a $2500 deductable. My personal insurance company provides $30 per day for 30 days for a rental car. It actually took 62 days for my claim to make its way through the bureaucracy of the insurance company and the bank that had the loan on my car that was totaled. This difference in insurance coverage cost me $2400. In 20 20 hindsight I would never been driving for Lyft if I was aware of this liability. If I had actually been earning any money driving for Lyft it was wiped out on the night of the accident.

Most other people driving for ride sharing companies, who do not have the misfortune of experiencing my discrepancy in insurance coverage, are still loosing money every day they turn on the app and they do not know it. They do not know it because it takes a lot of analysis to determine all the expenses of driving for a ride sharing company. Furthermore, since they derive so little of there total income from driving for a ride sharing company they do not have the incentive to do the analysis even if they had the knowledge of how to do it. The bottom line for the average driver is that they subsidize the ride sharing company because they do not generate enough revenue to cover all their expenses let alone get any compensation for the time they invest in driving for the ride sharing company.

In this book I will show that while drivers makes money only while they have a passenger in the car they incur expense for every mile they drive while working to earn money from ride sharing. While a driver may make $1.20 per mile while passengers are in the car, when the income earned is spread over all miles driven it can fall to as little as $.60 per mile. On the other hand, while immediate expenses such as gas may be only 15 to 20 cents per mile, when all expenses are considered, total expenses can be more then 60 cents per mile: thus, resulting in a net loss for every mile driven. Long term expense such as vehicle depreciation are just as real as gas expense, but may not be obvious until it is time to trade in a vehicle for a new car.

The focus on short term income is encouraged by the compensation programs used by ride sharing companies. Drivers can take their earnings every day in direct deposits to their bank account. This can be very attractive to drivers. The nature of the business is such that it is possible to make some money in any given hour of any given day of the week or year. The earning potential varies significantly over the course of a day or week, but there is always some demand for a ride. Unfortunately, all public utilities and transportation systems suffer from these significant fluctuations in demand for service. But, if you need money for some short term expense there is no quicker way to do this than to turn on the driver app and wait for a call for a ride, in spite of the fact that it might not be a very profitable time to drive.

When ride sharing companies first came on the scene there was a lot of anger from traditional taxi and limo companies because the ride sharing companies did not have to deal with all the regulation which limited entry into the market and added additional operating expense. This was unfair competition, which technical savvy people like myself thought was the inevitable cost of new technology overcoming the old technology. While this may still be true, the real unfair competition comes from the fact that the ride sharing companies operate with different Profit and Loss statements than traditional taxi and limo companies. The ride sharing companies also explained that they had an advantage because they had the technology to allow people to get efficiencies by sharing the ride. In 2018, ride sharing is mostly a myth and the numbers generated by the ride sharing companies themselves prove that ride sharing is a myth in the overall scheme of the industry.

During the dot com boom and bust many companies seemed to defy gravity and many reasonable business people really believed that I am losing money today but soon or latter I will may it up in volume. In reality, sooner or later the market place prevails and separates the winners from the losers. Investors have committed almost unbelievable billions of dollars into ride sharing companies. Uber currently has a valuation over $70 billion. Over the long run how long can ride sharing companies defy gravity?

Chapter 1

Unintended Consequences

Two of the biggest technical innovations of the last century, cell phones and personal computers, had impacts far greater than anticipated by the developers when they were first introduced. This is mostly due to the fact that the developers did not see all the utility that was in their innovation, because they were used in a way that they did not anticipate. This change in implementation is at the heart of why ride sharing is not really providing the economic benefits that people anticipate.

When cell phones were introduced they were big and bulky. They were used only in cars and the service was very expensive compared to land line phones. Due to these factors developers projected that maybe when cell phones were fully implemented there would be about a million users. It was anticipated that the only people that would use cell phones would be wealthy people that would use the phones to call their friends and business associates while they were being driven around in their limousines.

What really happened was businesses people who spent a large part of their day on the road started to use cell phones in spite of their cost to better use the their time on the road. They were in contact with the home office and they could call customers and suppliers from the road rather than wait until they got back to the office. The phones were expensive but they were less costly than the value of their unproductive time on the road.

Even several years later when it became apparent the cell phones were being more widely used than originally anticipated, planners at the telephone companies were designing equipment and software to integrate cell phones with land line phones, business and personal telephone. These services were going to be called Personal Communications Service (PCS). These plans and projections were being made by the premier research and development organization in the world, Bell Laboratories. Even the best and the brightest could not get it right.

The power of Morse law, which says computing power will double every 18 months, reduced the size and cost of cell phones dramatically. This fact combined with the fact that cell phones were marketed by companies that were in competitive market rather than a regulated market brought us to the world we know have today of billions of smart phones in the hands of a significant proportion of the worlds population regardless of income.

The second innovation was the personal computer. In the 1970s major corporations were introducing the use of computers to assist mangers with the computation and analysis of sales and production data that before that time was all done manually with pencil paper and calculators, or it was not done at all in many cases. The actual processing was done on centralized also know as main frame computers. In order for a manger utilize the services of the Data Processing (DP) he would sit down with programmers who would format reports and describe the data input and calculations required. The programmer would then go back to their cubicles and write the programs that would produce the reports. This process would often take months and once you committed to a specific report format that's what you got.

When personal computers were introduced they provided a viable alternative to this process. Mangers that were technically savvy could use personal computers to their advantage in competition with other managers that were not as technically savvy. At the time the price point for a personal computer was about $3000, which was also generally in the range of the amount that a manger could spend on his own authority, without getting approval from someone higher up in the organization. The personal computer freed the department manger from the delays and inflexibility of dealing with the corporate DP department.

The first personal computers were introduced by start up companies such as Apple and Comodore. At the time, IBM noted this activity in personal computers. Although it did not know how far this trend would go they decided that they needed to have an entry in the market sector. They projected that 400,000 units would be sold the first year. However, since IBM was entering the market they unofficially provided an endorsement of the personal computer as a legitimate business device.

Since the personal computer was not like anything IBM was already making, it set of a new standalone organization in Florida to design and produce its personal computer. The computer was made from off the shelf parts rather than proprietary parts which had been the industry practice at that point. Since actual demand came in at around two million units other start up companies such as Dell and Compaq produced very similar devices from the same off the shelf parts to fill the gap in demand.

A common factor with these two examples is the new product or service was not competing, at least in part, with an existing product or service, but rather it was creating a new market from the utility that was provided by the new product or service. This is also true of the ride sharing market. The resistance to ride sharing services is that it is competing with taxi and limousine services. This is especially true in regulated markets which have barriers and costs to market entry that are not the same for ride sharing services. However ride sharing services introduce technology that makes their operation more efficient and more reliable than existing taxi and limousine services. But technology is not the only factor that makes ride sharing so much less expensive than existing services. A very important factor in success of the ride sharing service is a new business model. Unfortunately, this business model has a serious flaw. It is difficult to calculate the true cost of the ride sharing service and drivers may unwittingly be subsidizing the cost of the service.

Before we go on to explore this point we should review what we know and don't know about the ride sharing market and its operations. We will talk about the US marketplace. Conditions in other parts of the world, such as China, are quite different and we could come to different conclusions for these markets. This is a very rapidly changing market. Thus, some numbers may have already changed, but the changes should not change the major conclusions.

The market in the US is dominated by 2 major players, Uber and Lyft. Uber has about 63 percent of the market and Lyft has about 35 percent. All the other players make up 2 percent. Anyone of these companies gets lost in rounding. Lyft is growing faster than Uber so currently Uber is losing market share to Lyft. The overall market continues to expand rapidly. Lyft operating mostly in the US and Canada, while Uber is a world wide player. The absolute size of either company does not have that much impact on profitability. However, the share of a local market can impact operating profits.

Uber has 3 million drivers and Lyft has 1.4 million drivers. Any driver numbers are soft numbers because almost all drivers are part time drivers to some degree. Both companies have people who have downloaded the Driver App and done everything required to accept rides, but have as yet do their first ride. Forty five percent of all Uber drivers make less than $99 per month, while only two percent make more than $1,500. Even on the high end, people drive to supplement some other income producing activity. This makes sense demand varies during the day so more drivers are needed at some times in the day vs other times. Driver turn over is high. Various numbers have been quoted, but one can be safe in saying that driver turnover is somewhere north of 50 percent per year. The part time nature of the work and the high turnover does not encourage any individual to take a hard look at all the numbers, when they are considering how much money they are making, if they are making any money at all.

Two factors that encourage people to become drivers are flexibility and quick pay. Drivers can turn on the app on any given day and make some money driving. They will make more money per hour at certain times of the day, but it will still be more than sitting in front of the TV. Lyft has a program that enables a drivers to have their earnings for the day deposit in their bank account, and be available in about 15 minutes.

Any published numbers on driver's hourly rate of pay are virtually meaningless. Any numbers published are simply a gross revenue generated by the driver divided by the time that the driver has the app open. It can be said that these number are highest number that a driver could achieve, because all revenue must be reduced by the drivers expenses to operate and maintain their vehicles, and the hours driving must be increased by the time driving to pick up a passenger and the time spent driving back to home base to either end the day or get in a position where the next ride can be accepted. For example, it takes about two hours without traffic to drive from the western part of New Jersey to JFK airport. That trip involves two hours on the meter to the airport and two hours or more off the meter returning to western New Jersey. A driver may make the return trip in legs, with an hour getting back to New Jersey and then picking up a ride in New Jersey, but It is almost impossible to get a fare paying ride back to western NJ.

17

Ride sharing have all the information about a ride while a passenger is in the car including time and distance traveled. They also share this information with drivers. However, they have no information about time and distance travelled on the return trip.

As in the case of wireless phones and personal computers there is a important factor that was not considered in the original projection of the business. In the original projection the assumption was that two or more people would be sharing the expense of traveling from point A to point B. The ride sharing software was designed to enable this activity. Unfortunately, the program has morphed into a program that enables a service very similar to taxi service. One of the riders has become the shared ride driver that bears all the expenses of providing the service and the other rider pays a fee that may not be based on the true cost of the service. Furthermore rates are set by two major corporations that are competing with each other for market share, with little or no input from the person providing the service. Furthermore, drivers do not have a understanding of all the costs they incurring to provide the service.

Chapter 2

History and Current Status of Ride Sharing

Carpooling or ridesharing has long been an effective way for people with similar schedules and work locations to help meet the demands of one another. This in turn leads to savings of time and money. Municipalities have established Park and Ride lots for people to park their car and then continue the rest of there commute with a friend or coworker. Some highway lanes have been designated as carpool lanes, which can only be used by vehicles that have at least two people inside. Less than 10 percent of all vehicles on the road have anyone other than the driver in them. Traffic engineers have calculated if we could increase the percent of vehicles on the road with 2 or more people to 40 percent all traffic congestion would be eliminated. More recently with the concerns of auto emissions contributing to global warming there is an added incentive for ride sharing.

While Uber and Lyft are referred to as ride sharing services, it is hard to find anything else that has been so inappropriately named. Uber and Lyft were established about 10 years ago to facilitate efforts for people to share their ride. But these businesses have evolved so that there is very little ride sharing going on.

Lyft offers a service it calls a shared ride. With this service when one passenger is in route to their destination the driver can divert from a direct path to the first passengers destination to pick up another passenger who is traveling to a point on the path to the first destination or to a destination some where close to the first destination. In consideration that the first passenger may be delayed by the side trip to pick up another passenger shared riders pay a lower fair than if they will be driven directly to their destination. In reality, most people select the shared rate because they see it is cheaper than the regular Lyft rate. Some people are not even aware that they may be delayed by a side trip to pick up another passenger.

In my experience driving for Lyft less than 5 percent of all people who are riding with a shared rate are ever actually diverted to pick up another passenger in the course of the ride. It happens so infrequently that both drivers and passengers can be confused at first when the navigation system all of a sudden starts changing the driving directions. Experienced Lyft riders know this, so more than 30 percent all rides are at the shared rate to save money. My experience has been that even when you are driving to a popular destination such as an airport the only passenger in the car is the first passenger. On a long trip to an airport the difference in the fares can save the rider up to $10.

Somewhat related to the shared rate is the Lyft destination mode. Often when a driver drops off a passenger at their destination, especially if it has been a long ride, the driver has to drive empty to get back somewhere in the vicinity of their home base. While driving back to home base a driver can select destination mode. When in destination mode a driver will only get calls for a pick up that are between their current location and their destination. Unfortunately, destination mode does not work that well. In the following example the scale is way off, but I am using cities in the example that are familiar to most people and more important they know the relative geographic position of these cities. While I am driving in destination mode from Washington DC to Boston, I get a call for a pick up in New York City, while I am driving through New Jersey. When I pick up the passenger in New York City, I learn that this passengers destination is Pittsburg PA. When I finish driving this passenger to Pittsburg, I am further away from my original destination than when I picked up the passenger. In any case, drivers do not get that many calls for rides while in destination mode, so it does make that much difference in overall driving efficiency.

Chapter 3

How Does Lyft Work

Enabling Technology

Ride sharing systems work so well that it is easy to lose sight of the truly amazing software and hardware that is used by these services. Furthermore, besides the Apps that actually delivers the service, which is a very small part of the unique technology used to enable the service, all the technology was developed for other reasons or services. In other words these services would never be possible or economically viable, if most of the technology used by these services was not developed for other reasons.

Smart Phones

The number of smart phones in use today is in the billions. There is no other device that has a greater penetration in the world's populations. In spite of the relatively high cost of these devices, everyone wants to own a smart phone. Thanks to the telecommunications carriers and their creative financing systems most people who can benefit from a ride sharing system have a smart phone that will allow them to a use a ride sharing service.

For the people that do not own a smart phone new services that can be accessed with a regular phone, such as Go Go Grandad, allow people to order and pay for an Uber or Lyft ride.

GPS Google maps

GPS or Global Positioning Systems were developed by the military to target weapons and other military activities that are involved with warfare. Before GPS systems became available, telephone service providers once provide yellow pages directories that could be used to locate and contact product vendors and service providers. The yellow pages business was a multi-billion dollar revenue generator for the telephone companies and some other independent directory publishers.

When people started using mobile telephones, is was a natural product extension to provide this information based on the current position of the person looking for the product or service. The cost of the original satellite systems were financed out of defense budgets and the huge cost of creating the service directories was justified by the huge advertising revenue that the service providers could get from companies that have products and service to sell.

Electronic Payment Systems

Taxis originally were an all cash business. The cab had a mechanical meter that calculate the fare based on the time and distance of the ride. The fact that the drivers had cash, exposed then to the potential of robbery. Taxis started to accept credit cards but they were still exposed to potential losses since there was no way to determine if a credit card was valid. Finally wireless payment devices were introduced to cabs which reduced credit risks. The one innovation that can be credited to the ride sharing companies was the systems that they developed that allowed them to calculate potential fares based on the pick up and drop off locations.

With the power of a computer now available the ride sharing service could introduce multiple rates and serviced such as a shared or dedicated ride. The actual fare can always be updated by actual information about the ride generated from the GPS.

Instant Feedback

Another innovation of the ride sharing system was the development of driver and customer databases. These databases are continually updated with feedback from riders on the performance of the drivers and in turn feedback from drivers on passengers. Although the whole service takes place within the confines of an individual bad drivers and bad passengers can be removed from the system based on excessive bad behavior. On an ongoing basis, drivers get reports of their performance as they are rated by passengers.

Requesting the Ride

In order to use the system both riders and drivers download a app to their to their smart phones. For drivers there is also a process of recording documentation such as vehicle insurance and registration information that qualify a person to be a driver. When the rider requests a ride the GPS system compares the rider's position with potential drivers in the area. Drivers and riders can be as much as much 20 to 25 minutes of driving time apart in areas where Lyft does not have many drivers. The system then sends out a notification to the nearest driver that indicates how far away the rider is in minutes of driving time and what kind of ride has been requested (shared or Lyft). The drive then must accept the ride in xx seconds. Drivers have an option of not accepting the ride, but the system tracks what percent of requests are accepted. Lyft prefers that drivers accept at least 90 percent of ride requests.

If a driver accepts a ride the system downloads turn by turn instruction to the pickup location. It also shows how long and how many miles to the pickup. . When a ride is over 45 minutes the system will show that the ride is at least 45 minutes in duration.

The driver only gets this information after the ride is accepted. There is one exception

When the driver arrives at the pick up location the driver sends out a message that he has arrived at the pickup location, The system will usually display the address of the pickup location. With a Shared ride the passenger has 2 minutes to get into the vehicle. Otherwise the driver can go on to the next pickup if there is one in the queue or drive to a nearby location to wait for the next ride request. With a Lyft ride, which can be scheduled in advance, the driver waits for 5 minutes before moving on if the rider is a no-show. On all rides the passenger has the option to call the driver to provide last minute directions. In a large gardenapartment complexes it can be difficult to find passengers. On Lyft rides the driver has the option of calling the passenger before moving on.

Driving to the Destination

Once the passenger gets into the car, the driver indicates that the he has picked up the passenger. If there is more than one rider this will also be indicated and confirmed. The turn by turn directions are downloaded to the driver's phone, and the time and distance to the destination. However, the destination is not indicated so it can be a mystery unless the driver asks the passenger where they are going.

During the ride the system will tick of the time and distance remaining to the destination. It also provides traffic information such as delays and alternative routes. This is the same information that a person using Goggle maps gets where they are using the app to navigate to a location.

When you arrive at the destination the driver indicates that they have dropped of the passenger(s). The compensation to the driver is indicated at this time. If the passenger uses the app to give the driver a tip it can be done any time after the ride and it will show up in the drivers compensation shortly afterwards.

Getting Paid

One of the most attractive features of the Lyft system is the way drivers are paid. Everyone is paid once a week by direct deposit into their bank account, if no special requests are made. During each day the system shows the driver a running total number of rides and his earnings for the day. At the end of the day, or even during the day a driver can request that the current balance of earning can be transferred to their bank account for a 50 cent service charge. Drivers that do a lot of driving spend a lot of money on gas. This system allows the driver to keep the amount of money invested in rides to a minimum.

In addition to compensation from each ride the Lyft organization has an ever changing incentive system that pays a bonus for a certain number of rides in a week a day or even certain busy hours. These bonuses can also be deposited into a drivers account on request as soon as they are earned.

Chapter 4

Are You Making Money Driving for a Ride Sharing Company???

Are You Working FOR the Ridesharing Company???

During my career I have worked in one of three basic modes. I have either worked as an Employee, a Consultant, or an Entrepreneur.

As an employee I was committed to work for a curtain number of hours usually in a specific place, which may have included working from home a certain number of days per week. I was compensated for my time with an hourly rate of pay plus benefits, such as sick pay, paid holidays, health insurance, etc.

I often worked as a consultant and performed many of the same tasks that I did as an employee. My compensation was limited to a fix dollar amount for the project or a rate of pay for a period of the time required to complete a task. In some cases, I worked as a consultant for longer periods of time than I worked as an employee. The main difference between these two modes was that the commitment of the company was limited to the time or tasks listed in a contract. Usually my only compensation was the dollars specified in the contract for the tasks listed. There were no fringe benefits.

For tax purposes an employee is reported on a W2 and a consultant is reported on a 1099.

I never worked in a service business, but there are many people who work as plumbers, electricians, auto mechanics, interior designers, etc. that charge for time and materials, but the bill is for a one time specific task. However, these people also have a truck, a place of business, and equipment required to provide their service. These costs are referred to as overhead. They are costs that they incur whether they stay in bed all day or work 16 hours per day. People that work as owner operators in service businesses are referred to as **self employed**.

The third mode of work was Entrepreneur. In this mode I worked developing a new business that provided a product or service. In my case these were new products and services. In this mode my ultimate compensation was in the form of net profit when my income was greater than my expenses. My accountant may have listed a nominal salary on the books of the business, but I did not receive that compensation unless the business had a net profit before the charge for my nominal salary.

Small businesses run by entrepreneurs are the engine that drives our economy. All new jobs are created by small businesses, and they introduce most of the new products and services that we see today. There is a great amount of risk in being an entrepreneur. Nine out of ten small businesses fail in the first year. They fail because they cannot generate enough revenue to cover expenses until there original investment in the business is depleted. Banks do not lend money to small businesses and venture capital firms only back people who have some really great idea or a track record with another successful product or service.

Many people have the dream of running their own business and being self employed. Thus, there is always a steady stream of people starting new businesses. In addition, some people who were employed by other businesses are force to try self employment because they cannot find work in large companies or in public service jobs.

Most people when thinking about drivers for ride sharing businesses would consider them to be either employees or consultants in the wider definition of this term. There are several law suites that involve ride sharing companies that concern whether people who drive for ride sharing companies are employees and should be regulated by the laws that cover employee compensation and minimum wages etc.

I believe drivers for ride sharing companies are really entrepreneurs. While it is obvious that they are offering their services as drivers when the sign on with a ride sharing company they are also renting their vehicle on a ride by ride basis to the ride sharing company. Like other entrepreneurs they will only stay in business as long as their investment in their vehicle will support their driving. In the worst case scenario this could be for a long time.

As we explain elsewhere here ride sharing companies really only operate in name only as ride sharing companies, since only a very small percent of rides really involve two or more passengers sharing a ride. On the other hand, a good case could be made to call these companies car sharing companies. Almost all people that use their vehicle for ride sharing also use their car to go to work, shop, visit friends, and all the activities that people who do not drive for ride sharing company do. Many people don't even keep track of ALL the expenses of operating and maintaining their vehicle in general. Practically no one even tries, let alone is capable, of tracking all the expenses that relate in part or in total to driving for a ride sharing company. This book breaks down these costs and shows that for may people driving for a ride sharing company is a losing proposition even before considering any compensation for the time spent behind the wheel.

There are some people who drive for a shared ride company because they like the experience. As this book illustrates driving for a shared ride company is interesting and amusing at times. There are times when waiting for a ride is less than exciting but on balance it is much more interesting than most jobs in retail or security.

Most people drive for a shared ride company for the money they can earn and the companies actually describe the work as a career. I believe that this is a fair description, because you are operating a business much more than just working as an employee. While you are in many ways acting as an employee of a taxi service would act, but you are also responsible for providing and maintaining a safe vehicle with proper registration and insurance.

The concept of a shared ride company has evolved. In the beginning, and even in some cases still today, a person driving from point A to point B will share their ride with another person who is making the same trip. This is also known as car pooling. Since the people sharing the ride in a car pool know each other in some way, such as employees of the same company, the sharing expense can be informal. In some cases there is no expense sharing with one person providing the vehicle and paying the operating expense.

Over time this concept has evolved to a business model, and I am choosing the term business model carefully, to be much more like a taxi or limo service. A complete stranger requests a ride to be provided by another complete stranger to go from point A to point B with a specific charge for the service and provides a means of compensation, other than cash, for the service. The term complete stranger may be a little too strong of a term, because the ride sharing services maintain bios and databases on both drivers and passengers. These databases provide security for all people involved and some sense of community. People are on the Lift or Uber are on the app somewhat like they are on Facebook or Twitter.

Stages

When a driver is working for Lyft, the app is turned on, he is in one of four stages; 1.waiting for a ride request, 2.driving to pick up a passenger, 3.driving the passenger from pick up to destination, and 4.driving from a drop off point to another staging point or home base. While driving a passenger from pick up to destination a request for another ride can come in. If this happens the ride is placed in queue so that when the driver drops off the current rider he immediately proceeds to pick up the new passenger. The only time that a driver is receiving compensation is when he is driving a passenger from pick up point to drop off point, or in stage 3. This is also the only time that a driver is covered by the ride sharing company's insurance carrier.

Kinds of rides

    Shared vs Lyft

A passenger can request one of two kinds of rides; either a shared ride or a Lyft ride. In other words, either a ride where there is the potential to have another passenger in the car paying a separate fare. There is a lower fare for a shared ride because there is the potential for the driver to divert to another point to pick up another rider. Shared rides are only available for single riders, because there has to be room for other riders if another shared ride is requested. Dedicated rides allow the passenger to schedule more than one stop during the ride. For example, a person could request to be picked up at their house driven to a bank. The driver waits while the passenger does something at the stop and then resumes the ride to go back home or to a third point.

Type of vehicle

Passengers have an option of requesting various size vehicles as well as two levels of luxury vehicle.

Down time and driving empty

There are three ways that a driver can be waiting for a ride; waiting at home or a staging area and not moving, while he is driving one passenger from pickup to drop off and while driving empty from a drop off point to a staging area or home base.

Chapter 5

Income, Expense and Profit from Ride Sharing.

Income

All of the income from ride sharing comes in the stage while a passenger is being driven from the pick up point to the final destination. This income comes from five sources; 1. the driver's share of the fare that the rider pays the sharing company, 2. any tips that the passenger either hands to the driver in cash or the passenger adds to the fare on the app., 3, reimbursed for tolls., 4. no show fees, and 5, bonuses paid by Lyft.

The reimbursement is at the posted rate for the toll. By using EZ pass a drivers can make a small amount of profit on the difference between the posted toll and the discount rate for using EZ pass. Unfortunately, not all bridges and tunnels have gone to a one way toll system. Drivers get reimbursed for tolls going to the destination. If there are bridges and tunnels with two way tolls the return toll is on the driver.

If a driver drives to a pick up point and waits the allotted time for the passenger and the passenger does not show up, drivers are paid a $5.00 or $10.00 no show fee. Unfortunately, passengers will cancel a ride while the driver is in route to the pick up point and the driver does not get any compensation. This was not a big problem for me, but I mention it in the spirit of full disclosure.

Lyft also offers incentives to encourage drivers to put enough time in during a week to get a bonus for a curtain number of rides given. For example, a $45 bonus for 30 rides in a week. The incentives are also offered in stages for example $45 for the first 30 rides in a week and another $30 for 15 more rides in a week. These incentives are important because a driver does not have to do any more driving, and incur any more expense, than he already did during the week. Based on my experience, base fares account for approximately 85 percent of income and the other 4 sources account for the remaining 15 percent of income.

Since there are different types of rides, and rides are driven over a range of conditions from city driving to driving on an interstate highway. My rides tended to be longer rides driven on interstate highways. Compensation for just driving is roughly $.88 cents per mile driven and $.12 per minute driving. The remaining $.20 per mile driven comes from the other 4 sources mentioned above. Obviously, the fare structure favors driving at high speed on the interstate highway system. There is one draw back to this kind of rides which I will discuss later. Under ideal conditions, which never could be achieved a driver can earn about $1.20 per mile driven. This would require all rides to be end to end and the last ride of the day brings you back to your doorstep. All the time spent driving to pick up a passenger, and all the time getting back to your home base reduces the actual revenue per mile.

I mentioned earlier that there was one disadvantage to highway driving. The disadvantage is that every mile away from your home base brings you into a population base that is less likely to want a ride back to where you started. While you are driving around town there is a good chance that during the course of the day you will not be very far from where you started and the distance between drop off and the next pick up will be small. For example, if you drive someone to a shopping center there is a good chance that you will pickup your next ride at or near the shopping center. On the other hand, if you drive 50 miles to a nearby resort there is less than a 10 percent chance that you will get a ride back to even close to where you started out. In most cases, it is not even practical to wait around for any ride n any direction.

The table below illustrates the impact of the percentage of time a passenger is in the car has on the net income per mile for all miles driver.

Table 1

The impact of the time a passenger is in the car on the revenue for all miles driven

% a passenger is in car	80%	60%	40%
Revenue per mile (all miles)	$.92	$.69	$.46

Expenses

The two biggest factors affecting the operating expense of a vehicle are fuel efficiency and the age of the vehicle.

Variable Costs

Fuel efficiency of a vehicle is straightforward the cost of a gallon of gas divided by the number of miles per gallon. The price of a gallon of gas varies from day to day and it is possible to buy gas for about 20 cents per gallon less if you buy at discount or off brand stations. During 2018 in my market the price of gas has been between $2.25 and $3.00 per gallon. For a vehicle that gets an average of 30 miles per gallon, at a cost of $3.00 per gallon that translates to 10 cents per mile. For a vehicle that gets an average of 20 miles per gallon at $3.00 per gallon that translates to 15 cents per mile. A recent study done by the AAA revealed that the average cost per gallon of regular gas was $2.52. The cost per mile for a vehicle that gets 30 miles per gallon is $.084 cents per mile and the cost for the car that gets 25 miles per gallon is $.101per mile.

The cost of gasoline is a very obvious cost of operating a vehicle when the tank is empty, you have to buy more gas or you are not going anywhere. Other variable costs are less obvious but still just as real. They include tires, brakes, oil changes, and miscellaneous repairs that occur on an unscheduled basis tune ups, shocks, etc… The older the vehicle you are operating the more likely these expenses are to occur. In the first couple of years these expenses are low because it takes some time for things to wear out. The key point to remember here is that as you are driving you are incurring expense for these items, but you will not pay for them until some time in the future. According to a study by the AAA these costs vary from 7.25 cents per mile for a small sedan to 8.45 per mile for a small SUV. These costs were calculated based on a five year average for vehicles that are driven 15,000 miles per year. These are variable costs so if you drive more than 15,000 miles per year you will spend more in absolute terms, but your cost per mile will not be that much different.

Fixed Costs

This part of the analysis can get a little tricky. In most cost analyses fix cost such as depreciation stay fixed regardless of volume. But, as we shall show miles driven does have an impact on fixed costs such as depreciation. Any one who has ever traded in their car knows that mileage in addition to model year is considered when valuing a vehicle. The key point we will illustrate here is that when you drive for a ride sharing service. The extra miles you drive for the service has an impact on trade in value, and the newer the vehicle the greater the impact. In affect, when you are paid for a ride part of the payment is a transfer from the value of the vehicle to your current cash flow, and is in no way compensation for your driving.

According to the study done by the AAA a small sedan driven 10,000 miles per year will incur fixed costs of $5,755. The same vehicle driven 1500 miles will incur fixed costs of $7,820 per year or an absolute increase of $2,065. The cost per mile goes down from 57.75 cents per mile to 39.05 cents per mile. It is important to note the cost per mile numbers. When we are spending 15 to 17 cents per mile we are aware of the cost every time we buy gas or pay for repairs. While we are incurring cost per miles greater than 35 cents per mile, we are oblivious to these costs until we try to trade in the vehicle.

Some Profit and Loss Examples

Table 2 **Profit Per Mile**

	Billable Percent	Revenue Cents	Profit per mile
	80	92.00	
		cost per mile	
Small Car Miles Driven	10000	57.75	34.25
	15000	45.18	46.82
	20000	39.05	52.95
Medium Car Miles Driven	10000	77.20	14.80
	15000	59.11	32.89
	20000	50.22	41.78
Large Car Miles Driven	10000	84.28	7.72
	15000	65.36	26.64
	20000	56.10	35.90

Table 3   **Profit Per Mile**

	Billable Percent	Revenue Cents	Profit per mile
	60	69.00	
		cost per mile	
Small Car Miles Driven	10000	57.75	11.25
	15000	45.18	23.82
	20000	39.05	29.95
Medium Car Miles Driven	10000	77.20	-8.20
	15000	59.11	9.89
	20000	50.22	18.78
Large Car Miles Driven	10000	84.28	-15.28
	15000	65.36	3.64
	20000	56.10	12.90

Table 4   **Profit Per Mile**

	Billable Percent	Revenue Cents	Profit per mile
	40	46.00	
		cost per mile	
Small Car Miles Driven	10000	57.75	-11.75
	15000	45.18	0.82
	20000	39.05	6.95
Medium Car Miles Driven	10000	77.20	-31.20
	15000	59.11	-13.11
	20000	50.22	-4.22
Large Car Miles Driven	10000	84.28	-38.28
	15000	65.36	-19.36
	20000	56.10	-10.10

The income numbers were developed based on my driving for Lyft over the first 10 months of 2018. During this time I provided 1025 rides and generated revenue of $13, 060. The 1025 rides were composed of a mix of rides at the Shared rate and the Lyft rate. Very few of the Shared rides actually involved rides where I had 2 paying customers in the car at the same time. In effect, the rate for these rides was a lower rate because one rider was getting a dedicated ride for a lower fare.

The cost numbers are from a study done by the AAA. The AAA study developed costs for 9 categories of vehicles starting with three size sedans, and including 2 size SUVs, a Minivan, a pickup truck, a hybrid car, and an electric car. Since most ride sharing involves small, medium and large sedans, we have developed schedules for just these vehicles. The costs are for new vehicles that were driven 15000 miles per year for 5 years or a total of 75000 miles. There are three cost tables;

Table 2 is for cars that had paying customers 80 percent of the time, which we believe is the maximum utilization that can be achieved give the nature of the ride sharing,

Table 3 is for cars that had paying customers 60 percent of the time, which we believe is possible in mature urban ride sharing markets where the driver makes a concerted effort to be efficient in the times he decides to drive,

Table 4 on for cars that had paying customers 40 percent of the time. This would be for developing markets and drivers try to drive during a variety of demand conditions. In other words the drivers worked during peak hours but also worked some off peak periods such as late morning and early afternoon.

Obviously, the size of the car has an impact on the cost per mile in many ways. The cost per mile for fuel is higher, and the cost for depreciation is higher due to the higher cost to acquire the vehicle new. We included three rates of driving for the vehicle during the year 10,000, 15,000, and 20000. This is total miles driven and not the number of miles driven for the ride sharing service.

A revue of these schedules will reveal the following. Driving with a small car is the most profitable. But even a small car does not make much profit at 40 percent utilization unless the car is drive at least 20000 miles per year. On the other hand driving with a large vehicle can only be profitable under ideal conditions. Utilization should be greater than 60 percent and total miles driven must be at least 15000 per year.

Chapter 6

A Word of Caution on Insurance

I learned a very big lesson the hard way. I have a good driving record. Thus, I tend to self insure where it is practical. I carry a $1000 deductable on collision and comprehensive rather than what might be considered the standard deductable of $500. When I started driving for Lyft I read that that I would have $1.5 million in liability coverage while driving for Lyft which seemed OK, since I assumed that I would need that insurance if I had an accident while driving for Lyft. What I failed to do was check what the other coverage was, such as the deductible for collision and comprehensive. It turns out Lyft's insurance company has a $2500 deductable, which is almost like no insurance at all for minor accidents.

My insurance company and most insurance companies in the last few years have been offering some reimbursement for the cost of a rental car while your car is in the shop being repaired. I live in a single car household in the suburbs. Without a car my life effectively stops. Furthermore, in addition to Lyft I use my car as a part of my daily income producing activities. So what may be a nice fringe benefit of their insurance program, for other people is an essential part of my policy. My policy provides for $30 for 30 days or $900 if you use it for all thirty days. Lyft's insurance does not provide for a rental car.

I was recently hit by a deer. Everyone told me I was not at fault. Anyone who lives in a state with a large deer population knows that it is impossible to avoid a deer strike at night during mating season. My car was totaled. Therefore, while I was not at fault in the accident, the difference in insurance coverage is costing me $2400. While I was driving for Lyft I received a little over $13,000 in income from rides and bonuses. As I pointed out earlier, a good part of whatever I netted from driving for Lyft was wiped out by this difference in insurance coverage.

Chapter 7

Not Just a Taxi Service

There have been a lot of stories in the news about the controversy over riding sharing services competing with taxi services in places life New York City where taxi's are highly regulated and the barriers to entry are high. In New York City the ability to offer taxi rides is restricted to people who have a taxi medallion. Due to the limitation that the medallion places on competition a medallion can have a value on the resale market that is in the hundreds of thousands of dollars. Unfortunately, for the existing medallion owners they are the casualties of new technology overtaking existing products and service. The Eastman Kodak Company, which was for decades one of the best managed and profitable companies in United States was overcome by the impact of digital photography and then eventually by the incorporation of high quality digital cameras in mobile phones. This was a one two punch that no company could have overcome.

As is described else where ride sharing is much more than a taxi service. The technology enables many more people to offer the service in markets where a Taxi is not economically practical. Also since the cost of ride sharing is so low compared to traditional service the market has expanded to compete with other parts of the transportation market. The report shows that these costs may be too low and not sustainable over the long run. But these services will still be used the rates will just come up a little.

Public Transit

While ride sharing services are not as cheap as public transit, studies have shown that people who would only use public transit in the past are using ride sharing services. Ride sharing is door to door and is available at times when public transit may not be available. In the long run I foresee that some municipalities may negotiate deals with ride sharing services to provide service coverage on little used routes on nights and weekends. It is not uncommon to see a bus that has a capacity for 50 plus passengers driving along a route with only a few passengers. This application would be a perfect application of the traditional ride sharing concept.

Car Rentals

When business people travel out of town they rent a car at the airport which they use to drive to the place where they are staying and then drive the car to visit the customer. In many cases the car sites all day in the customers parking lot and is only used to drive to dinner and the motel at the end of the day. In the past this was the only alternative since there was no public transit. Now, people can use a ride sharing service to get to and from the airport and to and from the customers place of business every day.

Service Loaners

Car dealers providing multiple services on a car where they are required to keep the car all day will now provide a ride back to the customers home and back to the dealer when in the past they provide a service loaner car or no car.

Food Delivery

Dominos Pizza is well known for the fact that they deliver. Other fast food businesses are starting to offer delivery service via a ride sharing service. Even when the fast food business does not offer the delivery service, customers will now use a ride sharing service to pick up fast food.

Drinking and Driving

Ride sharing services have become the designated driver when people are going out on the town. Besides the issue of drinking and driving people do not want to have to contend with parking at the restaurant or place of entertainment. Men do not want there car parked in the parking lot while they are at the Gentleman's Club.

Chapter 8

Part of a Larger Economic Trend

As we pointed out in this analysis, it is not that straight forward what a person driving for a ride sharing company is making when all expenses are considered. But the perceived income is high enough to induce people to try, especially when the companies guarantee a four figure earnings for the first month. However, one must wonder why so many people have become drivers for ride sharing companies. I my case I am retired from work that used to provide much higher compensation, but I still need to work to supplement my social security. The people that drive for a ride sharing company come from all levels of wage scale in the previous or other jobs. Many of these people have families and are trying to support them in part or entirely with the money they earn as a ride sharing driver.

One reason is that the barrier to entry is quit low. If you can use a smart phone, you have all the skills required to be a driver, assuming that you already have a valid driver's license. As we pointed out ride sharing companies use a great deal of technology in their business, but the true complexity of this technology is hidden by the very familiar user interface. People also have to have a reliable car or truck, if they live in a large part of the country where a car is essential to daily living. As we point out earlier people driving for a ride sharing company are really driving for a car sharing company. All you have to do is provide proof of registration and insurance and you can accept your first ride. Not withstanding the above two factors, I believe the growth of ride sharing has been prompted by the current economic environment.

There has been much said about the fact that the middle class has not participated in the growth of the economy or the past few decades. Real wages have stagnated and benefits such as health care coverage and pensions have declined or disappeared completely. While I was doing this analysis it occurred to me the growth in shared ride services is part of this trend. An important aspect of the decline of the middle class is that the trend is hidden. While people may have jobs, many people are not working at a job with pay that is commensurate with the there experience and capabilities.

I recently viewed a documentary on the economy of Dayton, Ohio. Many of the jobs that people used to have in the automotive industry, have gone away, as a result of moving manufacturing over seas. People who once had jobs at the auto plants in Dayton at pay rates in the mid $20 range are now working for a Chinese glass manufacturer that ironically open for business in the old auto plant. They are now working for pay that is in the $13 to $15 range, which is just above the poverty level. This report defined the poverty level as $24,300 per year.

Chapter 9

Recommendations

Currently the ride-sharing experience suffers from the fact that no one has all the information required to be the most efficient operator, but the system could be modified to do this. The GPS system could monitor drivers who had the ride sharing app on and also had passengers in the car and when they didn't. At the very least this would allow drivers to know there true revenue for all miles driven. This would provide a base line for expenses. If the driver is spending more per mile than he is earning, he should stop driving, unless he has some immediate need which motivates him to take a long term loss in exchange for some short term cash flow need. Drivers could also take steps to reduce the operating expenses such as, use a smaller vehicle.

Drivers could also improve their efficiency by not accepting rides, when the distance to pick up a passenger is over a certain number for example ten miles. This step will require some change in thinking by the ride sharing companies. Currently ride sharing companies do not incur any expense when the driver travels to pick up a passenger. Even their insurance does not cover this time. So in the interest of providing the quickest pickup time to passengers, ride sharing companies encourage drivers to pick up all passengers that request a ride no matter how far away they may be.

Another change in thinking will be to determine, what is the most equitable way of allocating rides to drivers? Drivers want to be driving with passengers in their car so they will take one as soon as it is offered. Traditional thinking is to allocate rides to drivers based on a queue, or first come first served. From the prospective of profitability drivers may not want to take the first ride that they are offered. The ideal ride from the prospective of profitability is a ride where the driver gets another ride immediately after the first passenger is dropped off at their destination.

We can use Newark Airport as an example of a high traffic location where a new allocation system could be implemented. Due the local geography and population density the largest proportion of passengers being driven to the airport are coming from the north. The next most likely direction is from the west. The south and the east would be the least likely. During high traffic hours there are literally thousands of people being driven to the airport, arriving on public transit, or driving themselves to the airport, where they will park their car, for the duration of their trip. At the same time, there are thousands of people on planes landing at Newark who will need transportation to their final destination.

I have included people driving themselves to the airport and people on public transit because under a fully implement system these people could also be passengers that could be allocated to a ride sharing service, if it proves more convenient and less costly than their current mode of getting to the airport. At the very least the two major ride sharing companies, Uber and Lyft should combine all drivers and passengers in one pool. If these companies cannot agree to a pooling arrangement, then one company may use such an allocation system to attract new drivers to their company. A fairly large number of people drive for both Uber and Lyft so I believe such a pooling system is feasible, under several scenarios.

Under the following proposal it could be possible to get back to the original concept of a ride sharing service, where two or more people share the cost of the ride rather than being a taxi service under a different name.

Under the current system ridesharing drivers are allowed to pick up a new ride at the airport just after they drop off the passenger they drove to the airport. If they do not accept this ride they have to get into a queue of as many 100 other drivers who are waiting to pick up a ride. These drivers will get rides on a first come first serve basis. I either case there is no way of knowing where the passenger is headed. A driver from north Jersey could get a passenger headed to south Jersey and a driver from south Jersey can get a passenger headed to north Jersey.

To start both drivers are happy they have a good fair for a long ride to their destination, but once they drop off the passenger they eventually face a long drive empty back to their home base, which could be twice as long as the fare paying ride. If at the start these two drivers could have swapped passengers both would be saved a long drive back and the driving efficiency in terms of earning would be much improved.

Under the proposed system all drivers in the system would have a county designation. All drivers from Warren County, which is in western New Jersey would be allocated rides for passengers who are headed for destinations in Warren County. All passengers for destinations in Morris County would be allocated to drivers from Morris County and so on for all 26 counties in New Jersey. The passenger app could be enhanced so that every passenger could see the current queue for their county. Thus, if these passengers preferred to share a ride they would see who the potential ride sharing partners are.

In New Jersey, Newark Airport is the best place to start such an allocation system, but this system would also work well in Morristown on a Friday night. Sports venues are another obvious candidate for such a system.

Appendix I

Why ride sharing companies will not use self driving or autonomous vehicles.

Putting aside all the issues relating to technology, insurance and consumer acceptance of riding in a vehicle that does not have a human driver, ride sharing companies will most likely not make a company wide implementation of driverless vehicles. This is due to the nature of the business in which they operate. Transportation companies face the same issues as other facilities based service businesses. They all face a significant variation in demand for service over the course of a day, week or season. These services require a significant investment in capital facilities. Power companies need power plants or dams to generate electricity. These companies have a base load capacity and then use other resources to handle spikes in demand. Electric companies will use gas turbines or other less expense resources to generate power during peak demand. They also set rate structures that require industrial customers to reduce demand during peak periods

One can safely assume that the motivation behind the development of driverless vehicles is to eliminate the cost of the driver. Almost from the first days of manufacturing efforts have been made to have machines do what people used to do. An added benefit of automation has also been to improve the consistency and quality of output. Once you get a machine to do something it should do exactly the same thing day in and day out. Furthermore, it doesn't have to take bathroom breaks.

In the manufacturing environment automation is added to existing manufacturing capacity. The machine simply takes over for the person that used to do operate the machine. Currently ride sharing companies do not own the vehicles used to provide their services. They are provided by the drivers.

It may be possible to develop a scenario where a driverless vehicle could make sense for a delivery company. If the company already owns and operates the truck or car, eliminating the driver makes economic sense. Assuming that a driver costs $10 per hour, eliminating one driver per vehicle would result in a savings of $20,000 per year. It may be possible get even more savings if the vehicles are used more than 40 hours per week. Savings of $40,000 per year are not an unreasonable assumption. If a company has to invest as much as $20,000 per vehicle the payback is one or two years.

There are some differences between a delivery company and a ride sharing company. The delivery company pays an hourly wage to their drivers and also incurs benefit costs and taxes that are directly associates with the drivers time. Eventually, traditional taxi companies may be the first companies to introduce driverless vehicles, since there labor costs are also directly associated with the drivers time. On the other hand, the cost of drivers labor is implied in the portion of the fare that the ride sharing company gives to the driver. The real wage for the drivers is what they have left over after they pay all expenses. If a driver does not have anything left over or does not cover costs, there is no savings in labor costs. Worse yet if a driver has not been covering his expenses the ride sharing company will loss the indirect subsidy that it enjoys when the driver bears some of the cost of providing the service.

Going back to the ride sharing company we have to make some changes in our assumptions. First we have to assume an investment in the vehicle of $20,000 based on current car prices. Lets use the same number of $20,000 more for automation for a total of $40,000. Calculating utilization is a little more difficult. Based on my experience there are at most 16 hours in a day when there is demand for rides. This number could be as low as 10 hours per day when peaks and valleys in demand are considered. The delivery company can schedule deliveries. A ride sharing company has to wait for passengers to call. Finally, an automated vehicle has to deal with the same issues as a car with a driver. There is the time driving to pick up the passenger and the time getting back to home base. The home base issue may be less of an issue if the vehicle can stay in the drop of area and wait for another ride. However, this is questionable. Bus companies that carry commuters go back to the yard during the middle of the day and return at the evening rush hours. Ride sharing also has very different demand cycles. Peak demand is on Friday and Saturday nights. If we assume that 60 percent of clock time is on the meter we save $15,000 per year for an investment of $40,000. This results in a payback of 2 years 8 months, if the ride sharing companies were actually paying drivers $10 per hour. If in reality, the driver only nets $2 after expenses the payback is now over 10 years.

Until now we have only been considering the costs incurred while the vehicle is being driven, either with a passenger or to and from a fare paying ride. These are real costs that incurred as a result of providing the service. Because almost all drivers are part time, the costs incurred for the vehicle when it is not being driven become part of the drivers cost for his personal transportation needs. However, in reality there is some time incurred when a driver has the app on and is sitting either at home or staging area waiting for a call for a ride.

When I was driving for Lyft there were many times when I waited 30 minutes or more between the time I dropped of a passenger and the time I got a call for another ride. These lengths of these waiting times are a function of the demand for service and the number of drivers waiting to provide the service. In rural areas there may only be a call for service every 30 minutes. If there is only one driver with the app open the wait is 30 minutes, but if there are two divers waiting the wait could be an hour. This wait time will be self regulating in the sense that if there are no calls for rides, some drivers will become discourages and will turn of the app and go home for the day or for some time until it get busy again.

When the ride sharing company owns the vehicle, all the idle time waiting for the next ride will be an expense for the ride sharing company. Trying to estimate this idle time is very difficult, and I don't think there is any way to capture this number with any degree of accuracy. Uber has 3 million drivers and reports 15 million rides a day or an average of 5 rides per driver. Lyft has 1.4 million drivers and report only 1 million rides per day or an average of only .7 rides per driver. Grab has 2.6 million drivers and 4 million rides per day or 1.5 rides per driver. DiDi in China has 21 million drivers and reports 30 million rides per day or 1.4 rides per driver. With out looking at the numbers in more detail it is hard to believe the Uber rides per driver per day. Especially when Uber also reports that 48 percent of their drivers earn less than $99 per month.

  In any case, we do know that drivers are part time drivers, and many people have signed up as drivers but do very little driving at all. In my own personal experience, when I devoted a full working day to driving, I usually had about 10 or 12 rides per day. In a best case I had several rides in a row in the morning and a few more in the row in the evening with the rest of the time idle. As would be expected there will be peaks and valleys in demand. If equipment is provided for peak times utilization will be low, and if equipment is provided for low levels of demand, automated equipment must be supplemented with cars with drivers during many of the peak hours of the day.

Appendix II

Interesting Rides

As I mentioned earlier, driving for Lyft is like speed dating. You get a chance to meet a lot of people over a short period of time. Today riding in a car is almost a universal experience. While many people may need a car to get to destinations, they may not want to have a car when they get there or they may not want to be responsible for sober driving when they are ready to leave.

At the time that I am writing this I have been driving for Lyft for about 10 months. These rides were interesting if not amusing at the time and some seem to be even more amusing with a little time to compare them with the everyday experience of being a Lyft driver. The tenor of the report became more serious after my accident and the issue with insurance coverage. In addition, I started to realize that I had determined that there is a serous economic issue with regard to drivers compensation that had to be addressed, but I felt that a little comic relief would still be appreciated by the readers so I decided to leave these stories in.

There has been at least one TV show that was built around the experience of taxi drivers. While many people take the time to talk with their driver as a fellow traveler done the road of life, there an equal number of people that allow the driver to fade into a mode of non existence and will say and do things while riding in the car that they would never want their friend and relatives to hear or see. So here are a few stories I hope you enjoy them.

Camping at the Go-Go Bar

It was a dark but not stormy night. I was driving in a rural section of western NJ, when I received a call for a pick up. I was already well beyond the zone of street lights and this call was taking me further into the darkness. At the time of this ride, I had only been driving for Lyft for about a month so this ride request was making me a little nervous. In every other ride up to this point, when I arrived at the pickup point there was some sign of life nearby such as a private residence, a store, or train station. This ride request took me to the entrance to a state park, at night in the winter time. This appeared to be either a nasty trick or the beginning of something that was not going to have a happy ending.

After I am waiting for about 30 seconds a car pulls along side and the driver roles down his window and says to wait here while he parks the car. I could see a little from my own headlights and more from the headlights of the car that just drove up, that we were in an area for camping with cabins for sleeping. There were 2 more guys in the other car. They all got into my car. These guys were all in their twenties. Even with my limited experience driving for Lyft, I could tell by their mood that they were ready for a night on the town.

When a passenger requests a ride they enter the destination into the system, so there is no need for the passenger to tell the driver where they were going. All the driver does is follow the turn by turn directions as the ride proceeds from one turning point to another. We were driving only a short while when one of the guys asked what I knew about a nearby go-go bar.

If you drive on Friday and Saturday nights you soon become familiar with all the dance clubs, go-go bars and gentlemen's clubs. If you keep track of the number of rides to each location you can determine the relative popularity of each of these locations. As the ride proceeded I shared the information I had gained from driving to these locations.

When we arrived at the destination and as they got out of the car I thought to myself that when they left home that night they were on a camping trip that just became a tour of go-go bars.

Lovers Quarrel

I picked up a couple in a part of New Jersey that is about as rural as you can get for New Jersey. Based on their speech and appearance I assumed that they were Chinese. If I were not for the fact that passengers enter their destination into the app, I would not been ever be able to understand that they wanted me to drive them to a destination in the borough of Queens in New York City. Under normal conditions without traffic, the ride would have taken about 2 hours but due to an accident on the interstate on the way, the ride was almost three hours in total.

Almost as soon as the ride started they started a lovers quarrel. I do not understand a word of Chinese, they were in the back seat, and I had to pay attention to the driving. But as the ride progressed I started to realize that a lovers quarrel is the same regardless of the language. She would say something in a load voice to him, he would respond in a load voice, and they would carry on like this for a few minutes. Then she would start to cry and then the tone of his voice would get softer and it was obvious that he was apologizing and he would eventually be consoling her. This would go on for a while and then things would get quite and there appeared to some hugging going on. If they were not in a taxi I assume that this could have progressed into some make up sex.

Unfortunately, after a while the level of their voice would be raised and we were off on another cycle like the one just before. He would raise his voice, she would raise her voice, the crying would start and the reconciliation would eventually begin. This went on several times during the ride. Fortunately, each cycle would be little shorter on the load part and a little longer on the quit part. This ride made me truly understand that regardless of our national and cultural differences we are all part of the human family.

Front Seat or Back Seat

With a regular taxi the passenger always sits in the back seat unless there are so many people in the group that someone has to ride in the front seat. With ride sharing the riding experience can be more personal. Not often, but occasionally a passenger would choose to ride in the front seat. In a passenger vs. a real taxi the front seat can be more comfortable than the back seat especially with a smaller car.

Regardless of the difference in comfort, when someone rides in the front seat it is a much more personal experience for the driver. The passenger always talks with the driver and is usually asked more personal questions. In these cases the ride is really life two friends sharing a ride rather than a taxi ride.

Does my boy friend love me?

I hope this does not offend anyone or make me appeared to be biased, but It was often very interesting what I would overhear when one woman was in the back seat of my car and taking on her cell phone to another woman about their love life. There was this one woman who was very unclear about how her relationship with her boyfriend was going. She was talking about all the mixed signals she was getting from boy friend about how serious the relationship was. She would say the he would say one thing and then do something else which appear to contradict what he was saying. Near the end of the ride she made a comment that required all of my self control not start laughing at what she said. She was telling her friend about some speakers that he had purchased and then left them at her house. She said that he needed them for some day in the future. I assume that he was a musician. In any case, she said "he wants to get his speakers back and I hope he is not going to sleep with me just to get his speakers. That would not be good."

You can tell a book by its cover

Some times my impression of a passenger will change significantly from the beginning of a ride to the end. On any day I usually picked people at the home and drive them to where they worked. If we talked about anything it was usually small talk about the weather etc. On a couple of occasions I had a big surprise when I saw that I was dropping off the young lady to her job at the gentleman's club.

One day I picked up a woman at a hair salon and drove her to her home. She appeared to be in her mid sixties or maybe 70. We had a very nice conversation during the ride. When we got to her home she told me that the ride was the first Lyft ride ever. She said that the lease on her car expired recently and she decided to stop driving since she had her 95th birthday last week.

About the Author

Like almost every other Lyft drivers the author does and has done many other things other than drive for Lyft. However, the author has worked with or consulted on much of the technology that makes a ride sharing service possible. For a major part of his working career he has evaluated new technology and the products and services that have used these technologies. The three major technologies are microcomputers, cellular telephones and electronic payment systems. He is the author of over 100 articles and book length reports on microcomputer software, telecommunication products and services and financial payment systems. In addition to his own consulting company, he has worked for several fortune 500 companies, and more recently for Telcordia Technologies.

www.ingramcontent.com/pod-product-compliance
Lightning Source LLC
Chambersburg PA
CBHW020614220526
45463CB00006B/2590